INTRODUCTION

This book tells about the people that are buried at the historic LaGrange Cemetery in Titusville, FL. It is meant to be a memorial to the people buried there. The book also serves as a way to preserve the cemetery as the weather has already destroyed many grave stones and in a few more years, many more stones will be completely faded and maybe even broken or gone and the descendants of the people buried there won't be able to find the graves anymore. With this book, the cemetery is forever preserved in its current state.

INDEX

ABDO

Talal Ahmad Abdo

Born: 1943
Died: May 1966
Buried: La Grange Cemetery

ABRAMS

Eugene Abrams Jr (Son of Eugene Abrams and Indies Raiford)

Born: Nov. 12, 1902, Thomasville, GA
Died: June 25, 1994, Titusville, FL
Buried: La Grange Cemetery

Father: **Eugene Abrams Sr.**, Thomasville, GA
Mother: **India Raiford**, Thomasville, GA

Siblings: Alex 1897 GA, Chilbass 1901 GA, Magnolia 1902 GA, Lula 1904 GA, India 1905 - 1920 GA, **George** 1907, Colony 1908 GA, Ethel 1910 GA, **Roosevelt** 1913 - 1939

Married: **Laura Bell Dickerson** 1903 – 1975

Children: Hubert L. 1927, **Earnest Earl** 1928 -1993, **Martha** 1939 – 1939, **Mary** 1939 – 1939

Eugene's sister India Abrams died Apr 13, 1920 at age 14 in Brooks, GA. Eugene's brother George, his brother Roosevelt, his parents Eugene and Indies and three of his children are all buried at LaGrange according to records, however some of the graves have not been found and do not have a photo because of it, they are probably among the many unmarked graves.

Eugene's sister Chilbass Abrams born Aug 1, 1903 married Rupert Sims, born Jul 2, 1904 on Dec 6, 1925 in Titusville, FL.
The parents of Rupert Sims were David and Annie Sims.

Laura Bell Dickerson Abrams (Wife of Eugene Abrams)

Born: Oct 29, 1903
Died: Nov 1975 (Age 72)
Buried: La Grange Cemetery

Married: **Eugene** 1902 - 1994

Children: Hubert L. born abt. 1927, **Earnest Earl** 1928 – 1993, **Martha** Jul 17, 1939 – Sept 17, 1939, **Mary** Jul 18, 1939 – Jul 18, 1939

Earnest Earl Abrams (Son of Eugene Abrams and Laura Bell Dickerson)

Born: June 5, 1928 NY
Died: Dec. 31, 1993, Brevard, FL (Age 65)
Buried: La Grange Cemetery

Father: **Eugene Abrams** 1902 - 1999
Mother: **Laura B. Abrams** 1903 - 1975

Siblings: Hubert L. 1927, **Martha** 1939 – 1939, **Mary** 1939 - 1939

Earnest is buried next to his parents. His twin sisters Martha and Mary who died as infants are also buried at La Grange though the graves may be unmarked and have therefore not been found by the author.

Martha Abrams (Daughter of Eugene Abrams and Laura Bell Dickerson)

Born: Jul 17, 1939
Died: Sept 17, 1939
Buried: Sept 17, 1939 La Grange Cemetery

Father: **Eugene Abrams** 1875
Mother: India Raiford 1881

Siblings: Hubert L 1927, **Ernest Earl** 1928 – 1993, **Mary** 1939 – 1939

Martha lived for only 2 months. According to records she is buried at the LaGrange cemetery. There are many unmarked graves and the author has not found Martha's grave.

Mary Abrams (Daughter of Eugene Abrams and Laura Bell Dickerson)

Born: Jul 18, 1939
Died: Jul 18, 1939
Buried: Jul 18, 1939 La Grange Cemetery

Father: **Eugene Abrams** 1875
Mother: Indies Raiford 1881

Siblings: Hubert L. 1927, **Ernest Earl** 1928 – 1993, **Martha** 1939 – 1939

Mary lived for only 3 minutes, according to records Mary was buried at the LaGrange cemetery. There are however many unmarked graves and the author has not been able to find Mary's grave.
Eugene Abrams Sr.

Born: May 1876
Died: Feb 08, 1930 (Age 46)
Buried: Feb 11, 1930 La Grange Cemetery

Married India Raiford Dec 5, 1895 in Thomas, GA

Children: Alex 1897 GA, Chilbass 1901 GA, Magnolia 1902 G, Lula (Lela) 1904 GA, India 1905 GA – 1920, George 1907 GA – 1981, Colony 1908 GA, Ethel 1910 GA, Roosevelt 1913 GA – 1939, Queen E 1915

India Raiford (Rayford) Abrams

Born: 1882

Mother: Harrill Rayford 1845

Married **Eugene Abrams** Dec 5, 1895 in Thomas, GA

Children: Alex 1897 GA, Chilbass 1901 GA, Magnolia 1902 GA, Lula (Lela) 1904 GA, India 1905 GA – 1920, George 1907 GA – 1981, Colony 1908 GA, Ethel 1910 GA, Roosevelt 1913 GA – 1939, Queen E 1915

In 1930 India was a widow, she lived in Mims, FL with her daughters Magnolia, Lela and Queen and her sons George and Colony.

Alex Abrams

Born: 1897 GA

Father: **Eugene Abrams Sr** 1876 – 1930
Mother: **India Raiford** 1882

Siblings: Chilbass, Magnolia, Lula, India, George, Colony, Ethel, Roosevelt, Queen E

Alex was living in St. Petersburg, FL in 1945.

Chilbass Abrams

Born: 1901

Father: **Eugene Abrams Sr** 1876 – 1930
Mother: **India Raiford** 1882

Siblings: Alex, Magnolia, Lula, India, George, Colony, Ethel, Roosevelt, Queen E

Married Rupert Sims Dec 6, 1925 in Titusville, FL

Rupert Sims was born on Jul 2, 1904, his parents were David and Annie Sims.

Magnolia Abrams

Born: 1902 GA

Father: **Eugene Abrams Sr** 1876 – 1930
Mother: **India Raiford** 1882

Siblings: Alex, Chilbass, Lula, India, George, Colony, Ethel, Roosevelt, Queen E

Married Bentley Cuyler Jr

Bentley Cuyler Jr

Born: Jan 24, 1895 Mims, FL
Died: May 2, 1937 Mims, FL (Age 42)
Buried: May 4, 1937 La Grange Cemetery

Father: **Bentley Cuyler Sr**, Monticello, FL
Mother: Kattie Alexander, McDonald, GA

Married Magnolia Abrams

More about the Cuyler family in the "C" volume

Lula (Lela) Abrams

Born: 1904 GA

Father: **Eugene Abrams Sr** 1876 – 1930
Mother: **India Raiford** 1882

Siblings: Alex, Chilbass, Magnolia, India, George, Colony, Ethel, Roosevelt, Queen E

India Abrams

Born: 1906
Died: Apr 13, 1920 Brooks, GA (Age 14)

Father: **Eugene Abrams Sr** 1876 – 1930
Mother: **India Raiford** 1882

Siblings: Alex, Chilbass, Magnolia, Lula, George, Colony, Ethel, Roosevelt, Queen E

George Abrams

Born: Oct. 12, 1906
Died: Oct. 23, 1981, Mims, FL (Age 75)
Buried: La Grange Cemetery

Father: **Eugene Abrams Sr** 1876 – 1930
Mother: **India Raiford** 1882

Siblings: Alex, Chilbass, Magnolia, Lula, India, Colony, Ethel, Roosevelt, Queen E

Married: Cooper Wright Dec 24, 1932, Brevard, FL

George's grave stone has the dates as 1901 – 1981, but the SSN record shows his dates as above. George's sister Indies Abrams died Apr 13, 1920 at age 14 in Brooks, GA. His brother Eugene Abrams Jr. and his parents **Eugene Abrams Sr**. and **Indies Rayford (Raiford)** are buried at LaGrange.
Indies' grave stone has not been located.

George's sister Chilbass Abrams born Aug 1, 1903 married Rupert Sims, born Jul 2, 1904 on Dec 6, 1925 in Titusville, FL.
The parents of Rupert Sims were David and Annie Sims.

Cooper Wright Abrams

Born: Oct 12, 1918 Reedsville, SC
Died: Jun 28, 1936 (Age 17)

Father: Sidney Wright
Mother: Daisy Poser

Married: **George Abrams** Dec 24, 1932, Brevard, FL

Colony Abrams

Born: 1908

Father: **Eugene Abrams Sr** 1876 – 1930
Mother: India Raiford 1882

Siblings: Alex, Chilbass, Magnolia, Lula, India, George, Ethel, Roosevelt, Queen E

Ethel Abrams

Born: 1910

Father: **Eugene Abrams Sr** 1876 – 1930
Mother: India Raiford 1882

Siblings: Alex, Chilbass, Magnolia, Lula, India, George, Colony, Roosevelt, Queen E

Married Joe Roberts Jul 7, 1934 in Hamilton Co, FL

Roosevelt Abrams

Born: Jan 29, 1913
Died: Mar 13, 1939
Buried: Mar 15, 1939 La Grange Cemetery

Father: **Eugene Abrams Sr** 1876 – 1930
Mother: **India Raiford** 1882

Siblings: Alex, Chilbass, Magnolia, Lula, India, George, Colony, Ethel, Queen E

Married Elvia Mae Abrams

Queen E Abrams

Born: 1915 GA

Father: **Eugene Abrams Sr** 1876 – 1930
Mother: **India Raiford** 1882

Siblings: Alex, Chilbass, Magnolia, Lula, India, **George**, Colony, Ethel, **Roosevelt**

Langdon Lee Abrams

Born: Jun 7, 1877 NY
Died: Dec 1967 (Age 90)
Buried: La Grange Cemetery

Father: Langdon S Abrams 1842
Mother: Armenia Southard 1849

Siblings: Bessie A, William, Edna, Cora, Robert

Married: Lavinia Abrams

Children: Adelaide Abrams

Langdon's daughter Adelaide married Charles C Rosche on Dec 9, 1908 in NY. His brother Robert A married Mary Emma Valentine on Nov 30, 1909 in NY. Mary Emma was the daughter of Theodore Valentine and Jane Terry.

Lavinia Abrams

Married **Langdon Lee Abrams**

Children: Adelaide Abrams 1883

Adelaide Abrams

Born: 1883

Father: **Langdon Lee Abrams**
Mother: Lavinia Abrams

Married Charles C Rosche Dec 9, 1908 in Nassau, NY

Charles C Rosche is the son of John W Rosche and F Miller.

Langdon S Abrams

Born: Aug 1842 NY

Married Armenia Southard

Children: Bessie A, William, Edna, Cora, Robert, **Langdon Lee**

Armenia Southard Abrams

Born: 1848 NY

Father: Elijah Southard 1800 NY
Mother: Nancy Southard 1807 NY

Siblings: Mary 1825 NY, Ruth Ann 1830 NY, Lavenia 1834 NY, Jemima 1843 NY, Fanny M 1846 NY

Married Langdon S Abrams

Children: Bessie A, William, Edna, Cora, Robert, **Langdon Lee**

In 1920 Armenia was living in Nassau, NY with her son Robert and his wife Mary Emma, also living there were her grandchildren Arnold R and Dorothy E.

Bessie A Abrams

Born: 1870 NY

Father: Langdon S Abrams 1842
Mother: Armenia Southard 1849

Siblings: **Langdon Lee**, William, Edna, Cora, Robert

William Abrams

Born: 1880 Dec

Father: Langdon S Abrams 1842
Mother: Armenia Southard 1849

Siblings: **Langdon Lee**, Edna, Cora, Robert

Edna Abrams

Born: 1883

Father: Langdon S Abrams 1842
Mother: Armenia Southard 1849

Siblings: **Langdon Lee**, William, Cora, Robert

Cora Abrams

Born: Oct 1887 NY

Father: Langdon S Abrams 1842
Mother: Armenia Southard 1849

Siblings: **Langdon Lee**, William, Edna, Robert

Robert A Abrams

Born: 1890

Father: Langdon S Abrams 1842
Mother: Armenia Southard 1849

Siblings: **Langdon Lee**, William, Edna, Cora

Married: Mary Emma Valentine Nov 30, 1909 NY

Children: Robert L 1925 NY, Dorothy E NY, Arnold R 1917 NY, Raymond 1916 NY

Coretta Abrams

Born: 1883
Died: 1950

ADAMS

Dallas Hilliard Adams (Doctor)

Born: Feb 8, 1883 Ala
Died: Mar 15, 1950 (Killed by car)
Buried: La Grange Cemetery

Father: Lenyar Adams 1859 – 1935 Gum Creek Cemetery, Glendale, FL
Mother: Octavia Garrett 1875 – 1968 Gum Creek Cemetery, Glendale, FL

Siblings: Andrew Paul 1880 – 1962 Homeland Cemetery, Homeland, FL,
Leonard O 1885 – 1959 Gum Creek Cemetery, Glendale, FL, Willie L,
Viola, John 1893 – 1977 Gum Creek Cemetery, Glendale, FL , Alto L (Half-
brother, Supreme Court Justice in Tallahassee)

Andrew Paul married Emma Darby.
John married Nora Belle Sullivan

Married **Lela Nevada Balkom** 1887 - 1971

Children: Lenyer 1919 – 1995, Nancy Ruth (married Williams)1923 - 1993,
Dallas Walter Jr 1925 – 1988 Oakhill Cemetery, Clermont, FL, Macy Veleta
1909 – 1986 (married Pike), Chlora Lee (married Battle) 1912 - 1998,

Catherine Odey 1916 – 1992 ,Olin Hillard 1919 - 1995, **Osler Balcom** 1914 – 1977

Chlora Lee married Joseph Randolph Battle Oct 5, 1935.
Dallas Walter married Jean Irene Vail.

In 1900, then 17 year old Dallas was living in Walton, FL with his parents and his siblings, his maternal grandmother Clara Garrett, two aunts Jennie Garrett and Mollie E Garrett and his uncle Henry A Garrett.

Lela Nevada Balkom Adams

Born: Nov 27, 1887 FL
Died: Apr 15, 1971 Orange, FL
Buried: La Grange Cemetery

Father: Walter Peyton Balkom 1849 – 1923
Mother Mary Catherine Lowry 1847 – 1915

Married **Dallas Hilliard Adams**

Children: Lenyer 1919 – 1995, Nancy Ruth (married Williams)1923 - 1993, Dallas Walter Jr 1925 – 1988 Oakhill Cemetery, Clermont, FL, Macy Veleta

1909 – 1986 (married Pike), Chlora Lee (married Battle) 1912 - 1998, Catherine Odey 1916 – 1992 ,Olin Hillard 1919 - 1995, **Osler Balcom** 1914 – 1977

Chlora Lee married Joseph Randolph Battle Oct 5, 1935.
Dallas Walter married Jean Irene Vail.

In 1910 Lela lived with her husband Dallas and her daughter Macy in Sandy Creek, Walton, FL. Also living with them was 11 year old Martin Straughn.

Osler Balcom Adams

Born: Mar 29, 1914
Died: Sep 28, 1977 Hillsborough, FL
Buried: La Grange Cemetery

Father: **Dallas Hilliard Adams** 1883 – 1950
Mother: **Lela N Adams** 1887 – 1971

Siblings: Lenyer 1919 – 1995, Nancy Ruth (married Williams)1923 - 1993, Dallas Walter Jr 1925 – 1988 Oakhill Cemetery, Clermont, FL, Macy Veleta

1909 – 1986 (married Pike), Chlora Lee (married Battle) 1912 - 1998,
Catherine Odey 1916 – 1992 ,Olin Hillard 1919 - 1995,

Married Amy Elizabeth Rodes Jun 8, 1941 in Brevard, FL
Divorce: Mar 1958 Brevard, FL
Married: Apr 1958 Lake, FL

Patrick E Adams

Born: Jan 28, 1920 Gravestone Jan 28, 1921 SSN
Died: Mar 22, 1982 Brevard, FL
Buried: La Grange Cemetery

ADDISON

Herbert Addison

Born: Mar 5, 1915
Died: Feb 8, 1990 Orange, FL
Buried: La Grange Cemetery

Married **Annie Bell Addison**

Annie Bell Addison

Born: Aug 29, 1928
Died: May 15, 2005
Buried: La Grange Cemetery

Married **Herbert Addison**

Madge Ferguson Addison

Born: Feb 10, 1906
Died: Oct 10, 1991
Buried: La Grange Cemetery

Mother: Mary Ferguson 1873

Siblings: Elizabeth 1913

Married **William F Addison** 1937 – 1990

Children: Billy 1938

William F Addison

Born: Jun 18, 1937
Died: May 8, 1990 Brevard, FL (Age 52)
Buried: La Grange Cemetery

Married **Madge Ferguson** 1906 – 1991

Children: Billy 1938

ADKINS

William Henry Adkins

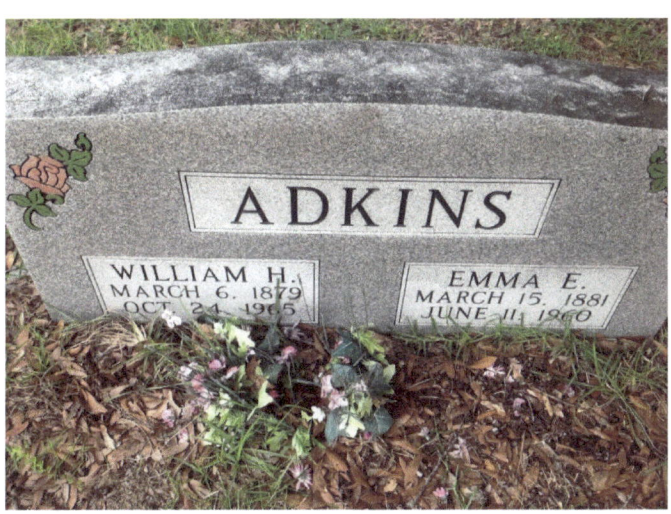

Born: Mar 6, 1879 Indiana
Died: Oct 24, 1965
Buried: La Grange Cemetery

Married **Emma Evylin Kemper** Sept 27, 1900 in Fountain, Indiana

Children: Lloyd 1905 IN, Lester 1907 – 1970 Lincoln Charter Township
Cemetery Stevensville, Michigan

Emma Evylin Kemper Adkins

Born: Mar 15, 1881
Died: Jun 11, 1960
Buried: La Grange Cemetery

Married **William Henry Adkins** Sept 27, 1900 in Fountain, Indiana

Children: Lloyd 1905 IN, Lester 1907 – 1970 Lincoln Charter Township
Cemetery Stevensville, Michigan

AKER

Ma…… Aker

Born: 1902
Died: 1983

Grave stone is broken and the first name can't be read

ALEWINE

Artemus J Alewine

Born: Dec 17, 1891 SC
Died: Jul 11, 1975 Brevard, FL
Buried: La Grange Cemetery

Married Ada Aquilla E Alewine

Children: Burke T Ricard 1910 (Stepson) SC, Ganelle D Alewine 1923 SC

Ada Aquilla E Alewine

Born: 1880 SC
Died: Apr 1962
Buried: La Grange Cemetery

First Marriage Noah Clifton Ricard 1876 - 1912
Second Marriage **Artemus J Alewine**

Children: Burke T Ricard 1910 SC, Ganelle D Alewine 1923 SC

ALEXANDER

Flora Lee Alexander

Born: Oct 31, 1916
Died: Dec 17, 2007 Brevard
Buried: La Grange Cemetery

ALFORD

Raymond Eugene "Gene" Alford

Born: Jan 10, 1950
Died: Mar 4, 2003 FL
Buried: La Grange Cemetery

Father: Raymond Alford
Mother: Iris Alford

Siblings: Robert Lee, Jane,

Married June 13, 1970 Brevard
Divorce: Mary Sept 5, 1995 Putnam, FL

Children: Raymond Eugene, Valerie, Bethany Joy

Iris L Booth Alford

Born: Mar 23, 1928
Died: Mar 13, 2005 Mims, FL
Buried: La Grange Cemetery

Married **Raymond Alford** Apr 7, 1945, Baker, FL

ALLEN

Herbert Lee Allen

Born: Nov 29, 1941
Died: Aug 25, 1982 Brevard (Age 40)
Buried: La Grange Cemetery

Horace Lee Allen Jr.

Born: Nov 10, 1945, Richmond, NC
Died: Feb. 28, 2004, Last residence Onondaga, NY, (Age 59)
Buried: LaGrange Cemetery

Father: Horace Allen

Robert Allen

Born: Oct. 25, 1914 Miss
Died: May 1, 2001, Mims, FL (Age 87)
Buried: La Grange Cemetery

Willie James Allen

Born: Apr 29, 1947
Died: May 4, 2009 (Age 62)

Buried: La Grange Cemetery

Married Brenda J Allen

ALRED

Samuel Franklin Alred Sr

Born: Jun 2, 1903 TN
Died: Jul 12, 1979 Lafayette, FL
Buried: La Grange Cemetery

Father: F M Alred 1864 TN
Mother: Mary A Alred 1874 TN

Siblings: John 1894 TN, Margaret 1896 TN, Roxie 1897 TN, Tolliver H T 1900 TN, Maudie 1906 TN, Son Alred 1908 TN, Edgar 1909 TN

Married **Oma Agnes Browning** Nov 29, 1925 in Whitesville, Boone, WV\

Children: **Norman Roy** 1927 -1977,**Samuel F Jr** 1926 – 1995, Tom, Ruth Ann

Oma Agnes Browning Alred

Born: Sept 1, 1905
Died: May 13, 1967
Buried: La Grange Cemetery

Father: Floyd Ribble Browning 1879 WV
Mother: Viola Pack 1883 WV

Siblings: Ada E 1904 WV, Ira E 1910 WV, Ester 1903 WV

Married **Samuel Franklin Alred Sr** Nov 29, 1925 in Whitesville, Boone, WV

Children: **Norman Roy** 1927 -1977, **Samuel F Jr** 1926 – 1995, Tom, Ruth Ann

Samuel F Alred Jr

Born: Oct 3, 1926
Died: Jan 16, 1995
Buried: La Grange Cemetery

Father: **Sam Alred** 1903 – 1979
Mother: **Oma Agnes Browning** 1905 – 1967

Siblings: Tom, Norman Roy, Ruth Ann

Married Violet Cooper Oct 13, 1944, Boone, WV

Violet Cooper's parents were Hillard and Ida Cooper.

In 1930 the Alred family, consisting of 24 year old Samuel F Sr, his wife Oma, also 24, 3 year old son Samuel F Jr and 2 year old Norman Roy, were living in Butler, Montgomery, OH. Living with them were three lodgers named Sam Kidwell 36, Ester Kidwell 26, and 7 year old Doris L Kidwell. These people were listed as lodgers but the author suspects that Ester was Oma's sister, and Sam Kidwell would then have been her brother-in-law and Doris was probably her niece.

Norman Roy Alred

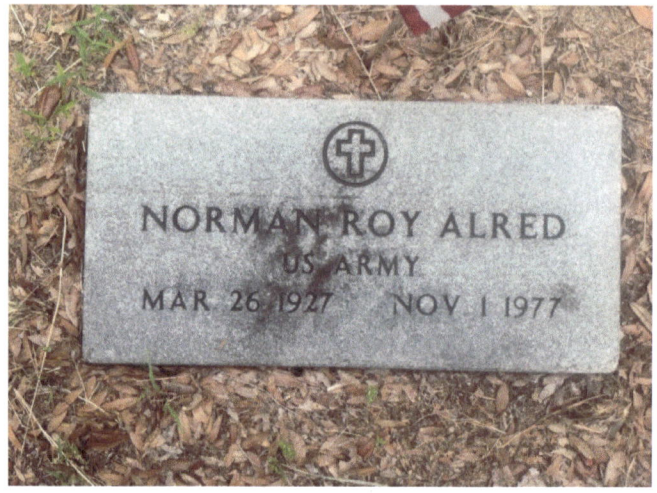

Born: Mar 26, 1927 Gravestone Mar 26, 1928 WV (Death Record)
Died: Nov 1, 1977 Columbia, FL
Buried: La Grange Cemetery

Father: **Sam Alred** 1903 – 1979
Mother: **Oma Agnes Browning** 1905 – 1967

Siblings: Tom, **Samuel F Jr**, Ruth Ann

ANCHORS

Frank W Anchors

Born: Nov 16, 1906
Died: Dec 13, 1982 Brevard, FL
Buried: La Grange Cemetery

Father: William F Anchors 1876 PA
Mother: Metta M Anchors 1879 PA

Siblings: Hugh W 1903 PA, Edgar R 1904 PA, Dorothy R 1908 PA, Kyle M
1909 PA

Married **Bessie Aline Griffis** Apr 2, 1935, Brevard, FL

Children: Rhea J 1938 FL

Bessie Aline Griffis Anchors

Born: Nov 22, 1927 Gravestone   Nov 22, 1917 (see note)
Died: Mar 15, 1999

Father: Nola Griffis 1888 FL
Mother: Nancy Griffis 1892 FL

Siblings: Sadie 1908 FL, Henrietta 1910 FL, Arnold 1912 FL, Nola 1914 FL, Oxford 1916 FL, Lucile 1922 FL, Violet 1926 FL, Grady 1928 FL

Married **Frank W Anchors** Apr 2, 1935, Brevard, FL

Children: Rhea J 1938 FL

Bessie's tombstone and her death certificate have the wrong birth year. Bessie was actually born in 1917. She got married to Frank in 1935 and would have been only 8 years old if the 1927 birth date were correct. She is listed in all of the censuses as having been born in 1917.

ANDERSON

Lena Mae Washington Anderson

Born: Feb 26, 1961
Died: Feb 27, 2003 (Age 42)
Buried: La Grange Cemetery

Lillie Pearl Anderson

Born: May 13, 1922
Died: Mar 26, 1989
Buried: La Grange Cemetery

Marian W "Gretta" Anderson

Born: Aug 23, 1916
Died: Jul 17, 2001
Buried: La Grange Cemetery

Nancy Wells Anderson

Born: Aug 25, 1942
Died: Feb 11, 1998 Brevard, FL (Age 56)
Buried: La Grange Cemetery

Paul Everett Anderson

Born: Aug 6, 1922 TN
Died: Aug 6, 1971 Orange, FL (Age 49)
Buried: La Grange Cemetery

Russell Anderson

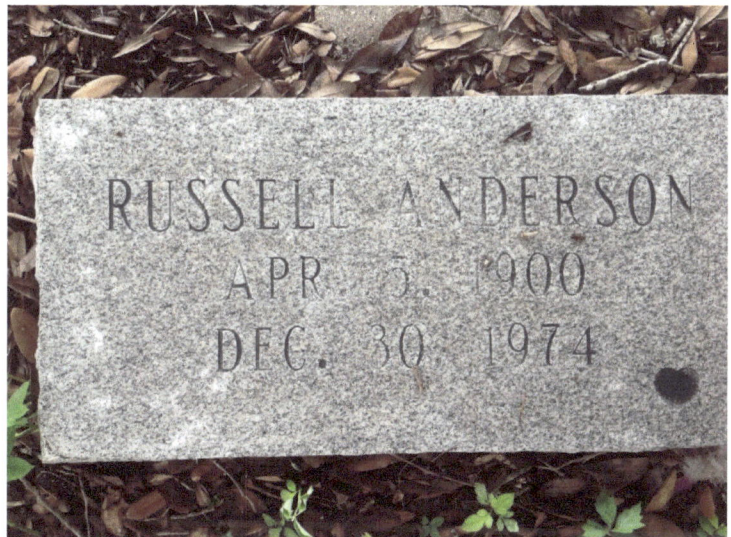

Born: Apr 5, 1900
Died: Dec 30, 1974 Mims, FL (Age 74)
Burial: La Grange Cemetery

Sammie David Anderson

Born: July 12, 1940, SC
Died: Jan. 12, 1999, Mims, FL, (Age 59)
Buried: La Grange Cemetery

Thane Hendrix Anderson

Born: Oct 6, 1903
Died: Dec 8, 1992 (Age 89)
Buried: La Grange Cemetery

Father: Henry Walter Hendrix 1873 – 1935 Providence Lutheran Church Cemetery, Lexington, SC
Mother: Minnie Rose Fields 1871 – 1911 Providence Lutheran Church Cemetery, Lexington, SC

Siblings: Henry Walter 1895 – 1962 Zion Lutheran Church Cemetery, Lexington, SC, Catherine Ann 1899 – 1901 Providence Lutheran Church Cemetery, Lexington, SC, Grace Adelaide (married Wingard) 1901 – 1995 Pilgrim Lutheran Church Cemetery, Lexington, SC, John Jacob 1907 – 1978, Providence Lutheran Church Cemetery, Lexington, SC, W W 1910 – 1911 Providence Lutheran Church Cemetery, Lexington, SC

Vivian Y Anderson

Born: Nov 23, 1954
Died: July 9, 2011
Buried: La Grange Cemetery

ANDRE

August H Andre

Born: Sept 11, 1881 Germany
Died: Jul 1960
Buried: La Grange Cemetery

Immigrated Apr 6, 1904 from Bremen, Germany to New York on board the Kaiser Wilhelm II

Married Helen A Andre

Children: **Arthur H** 1918 – 2010, **Herbert Frederick** 1913 Canada– 1945, Minnie A 1916, Montana Barthold V 1920 Vermont, Richard Harold 1922, DC

Helen A Andre

Born: 1891 PA

Married **August H Andre**

Children: **Arthur H** 1918 – 2010, **Herbert Frederick** 1913 Canada– 1945, Minnie A 1916, Montana Barthold V 1920 Vermont, Richard Harold 1922, DC

Herbert Frederick Andre

Born: May 18, 1913
Died: Aug 1, 1945

Father: **August H Andre** 1882 Germany
Mother: Helen A Andre 1891 PA

Siblings: **Arthur H** 1918 – 2010, Minnie A 1916, Montana Barthold V 1920 Vermont, Richard Harold 1922, DC

Arthur H Andre

Born: May 13, 1918
Died: Dec 24, 2010 Mims, FL
Buried: La Grange Cemetery

Father: **August H Andre** 1882 Germany
Mother: Helen A Andre 1891 PA

Siblings: **Herbert Frederick** 1913 Canada– 1945, Minnie A 1916, Montana
Barthold V 1920 Vermont, Richard Harold 1922, DC

ANDREW

Ervin Howard Andrew

Born: Aug 17, 1930
Died: Oct 8, 1962
Buried: La Grange Cemetery

Father: Ulna Andrew 1893 TN
Mother: Minnie L Andrew 1894 TN

Siblings: Nannie Sue 1922 TN, Thomas L 1924 TN

ANDREWS

John Rederick Andrews

Born: Jan 21, 1870 Ala
Died: Feb 10, 1934 Daytona, FL (Age 64)
Buried: La Grange Cemetery

Father: John P Andrews
Mother: Jane Burke

Married **Eola C Pelham**

Children: Melba H (married Stickney) 1909 – 1986 Roselawn Cemetery, Talahassee, FL, Alma (married Flood) 1900 – 1985 Arlington Park Cemetery, Jacksonville, FL, John P, Abner B, Julia Lois 1895 – 1898 Pinckard Cemetery, Pinckard, Alabama, Bowen Edward 1906 – 1978 Arlington Park Cemetery, Jacksonville, FL

Eola C Pellum Andrews

Born: Jan 21, 1870 Alabama
Died: Apr 25, 1960

Father: Charles Seawright Pellum 1820 – 1898
Mother: Julia Ann Arnold 1832 – 1899

Siblings: Rhydonia Costello (married Burke) 1851 1936, Alonzo 1854 –
1939, Columbus Seawright 1856 – 1857, Uriah Joseph 1858 - 1925,
Charles Bartow 1861 – 1865, Abner 1865 – 1875, Willie Osta 1868 – 1869,
Theophilus 1872 – 1873, Elie Nora (married Hrabowski)1876 - 1952

Married **John Rederick Andrews**

Children: **Freddie Pansy** (married Kyzer) 1892 – 1964, Melba H (married
Stickney) 1909 – 1986 Roselawn Cemetery, Talahassee, FL, Alma
(married Flood) 1900 – 1985 Arlington Park Cemetery, Jacksonville, FL,
John P, Abner B, Julia Lois 1895 – 1898 Pinckard Cemetery, Pinckard,
Alabama, Bowen Edward 1906 – 1978 Arlington Park Cemetery,
Jacksonville, FL

Freddie Pansy Andrews Kyzer

Born: Dec 30, 1892
Died: Nov 6, 1964

Father: **John Rederic Andrews** 1870 - 1934
Mother: **Eola Clee Pelham** 1870 - 1960

Siblings: Melba H (married Stickney) 1909 – 1986 Roselawn Cemetery, Talahassee, FL, Alma (married Flood) 1900 – 1985 Arlington Park Cemetery, Jacksonville, FL, John P, Abner B, Julia Lois 1895 – 1898 Pinckard Cemetery, Pinckard, Alabama, Bowen Edward 1906 – 1978 Arlington Park Cemetery, Jacksonville, FL

Married **Mitchell Oliver Kyzer** 1891 - 1943

Children: **Lawrence M** 1916 – 1953, Iris Eola (married Treadwell) 1920 – 2015 Oaklawn Cemetery, Jacksonville, FL

More about the Kyzer family in the "K" volume.

Sara B Andrews Singleton

Born: 1823
Died: 1895
Buried: La Grange Cemetery

Married Robert Singleton

Children: **Robert Morris** 1870 Louisiana – 1918, **Lyman Henry** 1876 La Grange – 1928

Robert Singleton

Born: Louisiana

Married **Sara B Andrews**

Children: **Robert Morris** 1870 Louisiana – 1918, **Lyman Henry** 1876 La Grange - 1928

Robert Morris Singleton

Born: 1870 Louisiana
Died: Jul 1, 1918 La Grange, Brevard, FL (Killed by Lightning)
Buried: Jul 12, 1918 La Grange Cemetery

Father: **Robert Singleton**
Mother: **Sara B Andrews**

Siblings: **Lyman Henry** 1876 – 1928

Married **Ovieda Simmons** 1886 - 1914

Lyman Henry Singleton

Born: 1876 La Grange
Died: Mar 16, 1928
Buried: Mar 19, 1928 La Grange Cemetery

Father: **Robert Singleton**
Mother: **Sara B Andrews**

Siblings: **Robert Morris** 1870 – 1918

More about the Singleton family in the "S" volume

Carrie Goodwin Andrews

Born: Dec 12, 1867
Died: Sept 29, 1915
Buried: La Grange Cemetery

ANESES

Aida Aneses

Born: Aug 4, 1937   Sept 21, 1937
Died: Mar 25, 2004
Buried: La Grange Cemetery

ARCOLEO

Umberto T Arcoleo

Born: Mar 24, 1916 NJ
Died: Jun 27, 1990
Buried: La Grange Cemetery

Military Enlistment Dec 16, 1941, Newark, NJ

ARNOLD

Peter James Arnold

Born: Feb 28, 1921
Died: Mar 30, 2011
Buried: La Grange Cemetery

Married Doris E Arnold Jul 12, 1942

Children: Warren 1950 – 1950

Military Enlistment Sept 26, 1942, Cp Blanding, FL, WWII

Warren Arnold

Born: 1950
Died: Sept 29, 1950
Buried: La Grange Cemetery

Edson Franklin Arnold

Born: Mar 21, 1909 FL
Died: Mar 5, 1969
Buried: La Grange Cemetery

Father: E W Arnold 1881 NY
Mother: L M Arnold 1888 NY

Siblings: Clara 1907 FL

Married Jeannette R Whidden Apr 21, 1935, FL

Children: Barbara W Arnold 1939 FL

Jeannette R Whidden Arnold

Born: Dec 4, 1914 FL
Died: Jan 5, 1959
Buried: La Grange Cemetery

Father: Archie Whidden 1870 FL
Mother: Lillian Terryn 1890 ILL

Siblings: Woodrow 1913 FL, Lorena 1918 FL, George 1924 FL

Married Edson Franklin Arnold Apr 21, 1935, FL

Children: Barbara W 1939 FL

Archie Whidden married Lillian Terryn Feb 8, 1910 in Escambia, FL

ATKINS

Bonnie Mae Atkins

Born: Oct 4, 1917
Died: Apr 16, 1980
Buried: La Grange Cemetery

Shares gravestone with Ida Rowena Grant 1884 – Feb 1967
(May be her mother?......)

ATKINSON

James Kenneth Atkinson

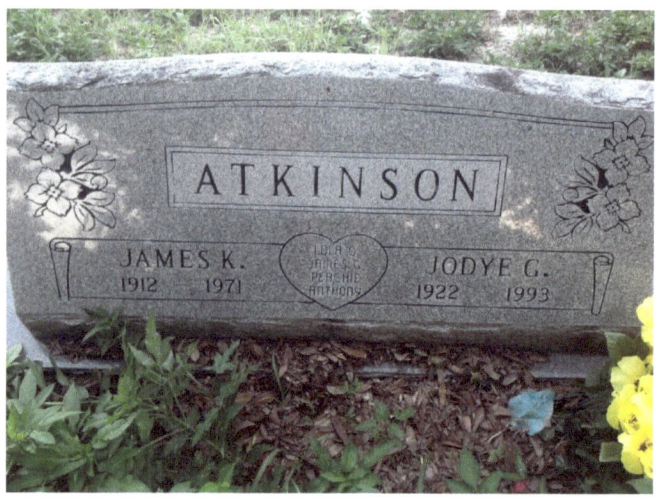

Born: Sept 29, 1912 FL
Died: May 1, 1971 Brevard, FL
Buried: La Grange Cemetery

Married **Jodye Garrett Atkinson**

Jodye Bell Garrett Atkinson

Born: Feb 7, 1922
Died: Jun 25, 1993 Titusville, FL
Buried: La Grange Cemetery

Married **James Kenneth Atkinson**

AUSTIN

William Spurgeon "Pappy" Austin

Born: Feb 6, 1910 Daleville, Alabama
Died: Jul 8, 1998
Buried: La Grange Cemetery

Father: June Arter Austin b. Apr 6, 1887 Alabama
Mother: Ila Johnson (Johnston) 1891

Siblings: Louie F 1914, J F (M), Cedric 1916, John 1921, Frances 1923,
Cedric 1919

Married **Polly F Austin**

Children: **Gerald Lee Austin** 1935 – 2006

Polly F Austin

Born: Nov 19, 1912 Alabama
Died: Nov 14, 1978 Mims, FL
Buried: La Grange Cemetery

Married **William Spurgeon "Pappy" Austin**

Children: **Gerald Lee Austin** 1935 – 2006

Gerald Lee Austin

Born: Dec 31, 1935
Died: Sept 13, 2006
Buried: La Grange Cemetery

Father: **William Spurgeon "Pappy" Austin** 1910 – 1998
Mother: **Polly F Austin** 1912 – 1978

Married Loretta L Austin

Steven Wayne Austin

Born: Apr 25, 1956
Died: Sept 29, 1985 Brevard, FL
Buried: La Grange Cemetery